# A Little History of My Life and Times
## Alexander Cecil Roy

For information on this book please contact RichardGerardi@yahoo.com
Copyright 2008

# ALEXANDER CECIL ROY

A LITTLE HISTORY OF MY LIFE AND TIMES

## ❋ 1916 was a special year ❋

*"The year when I entered this world! When I leave it, I hope to be remembered for whatever good deeds I might have done."*

It was the year 1916. English rule was causing destruction all over Ireland. At that time England was ruling there and Ireland was part of the British Empire.

It was 1916 that I was born – my birth place was 21 Connaught Place, Wellington Road, in Cork City, Ireland. My parents: my mother, Frances Cole, married to my father, Walter Roy. My sister, Betty, born 4 years before me, lived as I did, in the house on Wellington Road.

At this point of my story, I should explain. My grandfather, Alfred Cole, and my grandmother, Elizabeth, owned the house. We had a large family living there then – my aunt Dorothea, married to my uncle, Michael O'Riordan. Their two daughters Rita and Minie. My mother, maiden name Francis Cole, who died at the early age of 28 years, was married to Walter Roy, my father, an actor and play-write in London. My father traveled a lot in the world of the theatre and visited Ireland as often as possible.

*Cork - Taken by Brenda on a recent visit*

*May's Sunflower*

Very old Tin Type photos

*My Grandmother and Grandfather*
*Alfred and Elizabeth Cole*

*My Mom and Dad*
*Walter and Francis Roy*
*Late 1800's*

# My father wrote many plays and acted in many more. He was born in Scotland

*GLASGOW–Scotland.*
*My father wrote many plays and acted in many more – He was born in Scotland.*

*← MY FATHER*

Padre: *What makes cows in a field run after railway trains?*
The Padre has to repeat the first question to Dr. Macadam who is somewhat hard of hearing, when the oddly assorted Brains Trusters are launched on their perilous session.

*London*

## Scenes from "It Depends What Yo[u Mean]"

THE new comedy by the brilliant Scottish doctor dramatist, James Bridie, *It Depends What You Mean*, which has been unanimously hailed by the critics, is enjoying a well-deserved success at the Westminster Theatre where it is presented by Robert Donat in association with Merlith Productions.

The unusual title of the play gives some clue to its theme. An Army Padre (Alastair Sim) organises a Brains Trust for the amusement and edification of the Forces in an Army recreation hut in North Britain. With the inimitable Bridie humour we see what happens to private lives when the village wiseacres start answering questions a little too frankly. The leading question—"Is Marriage a good idea?"—is put to the Brains Trust by Private Jessie Killigrew (Margaret Barton) of the A.T.S., and she insists upon having a truthful answer so that she may make up her mind whether or not to marry her boy friend, Private Walter Geikie (Alec Faversham) of the R.A.S.C. Her question involves some embarrassment for the members of the Brains Trust. In particular, Angela Prout (Angela Baddeley) and her artist husband George Prout (Wilfred Hyde White), whose private lives are made public property.

Other members of the village Brains Trust are Professor James Mutch (Oliver Johnstone); Viscountess Dodd, the local Lady Bountiful (Nuna Davey); Joe Byres, a Scottish Labour M.P. (Walter Roy); and Dr. Hector Macadam, a somewhat deaf doctor (O. B. Clarence).

The play has been produced by Alastair Sim.

My Grandmother
Elizabeth Cole
I loved her very much
He's kind - Gone forever!
A wonderful lady.

*Late 1800's*
*She died in the 1930's*

My Grandfather Grandmother + Baby
I don't know? (Back of this picture is
a photograph of my mother as a baby,
I think - I couldn't remove it!

*Late 1800's*

Granny - Minnie - Aunty Teen - ABC Cafe Youghal about 1930!

*ABC Cafe was my grandmothers and had a bungalow on the side where we visited from Cork every summer*

*A theatre group. My mother is laying down in the front row.
This was taken sometime in the late 1800's*

*Picture taken in the garden in Cork city*

*Minie Walsh*

I had an Aunt Minie, who married a Belgium officer, and lived in Berlin after World War I. Anton and Minie Bayczinsky were both killed in a World War II air raid on Berlin, their daughters, Viga, Elsa, and May, survived.

Back in 21 Connaught Place, my Aunt Teen and Uncle Michael's daughters, Rita and Mine, went to school in Cork City. Later to marry, Rita married Tone Coughlan, native of Skittereen. From Cork City they both went to America and their children were born there – Alfred, Dorathea, Maureen, and Justin.

When my mother died, my grandmother and aunt took care of my sister, Betty, and I through our young years. In "21" in those days, we sure had a full house!

My grandfather, Alfred, with two partners, Alcox and Brown, had a grocery store, "Alcox", in the city of Cork. My grandfather also had a restaurant in the town of Youghal County, Cork. He called it the A.B.C. café (Alcox, Brown, and Cole). After his death, my aunt ran it for many years. Then my sister, Betty, took it over. After that. it was rented out for the summer months. Over the "ABC" was a bungalow, where my family and I spent many happy times during the summers – but that is another part of my story.

*1946 The Coughlan Family*
*Tone, Rita, Dorathea, Maureen & Justin*
*Missing is Alfred*

My cousin Minie, Betty and I called ourselves the "Three Musketeers". We were very close and helped each other in many ways.

*Justin Coughlan*

The years go by, Minie goes to the Urseline Convent School, Betty to follow a few years later and I went to the Christian Brothers College in Cork. In the evenings, I went to art class and Minie and Betty went to The Shakespeare Society. I joined for a while. In the 1930s approximately, I study and photograph with a photography studio in Cork.

If I am deviating from time to time it is because I am writing my story as I keep remembering things.

Time passes…Betty married Mick Ahern in Youghal…Minie married Leonard Walsh in Dublin. They have four children – Moira, Therese, Aiden, and Cecil. My sister and her husband didn't have children. So, my Aunt Teen (after my grandfather, grandmother and Uncle Michael died) kept "21" for a few years. I went to work as a photographer in London about 1936. My aunt Teen stayed with my cousin Minie and Leonard in Dublin, visiting Rita and husband, Tone, in Bray from time to time. Rita's husband managed a company in London – The "Block Drug Co." Then in America, Rita, Tone, and family lived in New Jersey, then they moved to Bray County. While Tone managed a company in London, Minie was in Dublin, Betty in Youghal, and I was in London. In 1939, war clouds were over Europe and Tone and family moved to Ireland.

Adolph Hitler invades Poland, peace fails, and war starts. I'm working in Scotland at the time. I join the "A.R.P." (Air Raid Precautions). After six months, I get called up to join the Royal Air Force.

*Auntie Teen - April 1934*
*Holding a Picture of Alfred Coughlan*

Betty, Minie, and I – "The Three Musketeers"- were separated and life would never be the same again. Remembering my young days in the little seaside town of Youghal, happy days then. I remember as a boy, enjoying my finds in the town, swimming and walking along the fine beach. Fishing off the "Green Park", going on many trips to "Monatrae". It could be reached by car or across the bay by boat. The "Monatrae Hotel" had many evenings of dancing, it also had a horse riding school. In the days when the trains ran from Cork – a distance of 30 miles to Youghal – they had what they called "The Sea Breeze Excursions" and for one shilling one could spend the day and take the last train – I am back to the city…bands on the promenade, singing on the promenade and the lifeboat dances at the "ballroom at the edge of the Atlantic". My friend, Bob Atkins, ran it then. My cousins, "The Pratts", lived in the town and while my grandmother was in the "bungalow" the family would visit from time to time. They were my young days and Youghal was my favorite place in the summer.

*Betty and Minie about 1928*       *Betty and I in Youghal about 1928*

*A friend, Betty (center) and a good friend Marie-
Early years in the late 1030's
Youghal, Cork*

*Betty, around 1941
Youghal, Cork*

*Betty, around 1939
Youghal, Cork*

*Betty and Minie about 1928*

*Betty (about 12 years)*

Sister Betty on Youghal Strand

Aunty Teen & Betty Youghal

Mick - Friend - Betty - my friend Miles Watson - & Jr Monatrae - Youghal

*Co Cork, Ireland 1930's*

*Sister Betty - Mick Ahern and Auntie Teen about 1928*

*An old friend Philip Lynch and I about 1940 - He later became a doctor*

*Chatham Seaport in England about 1940*
*I worked there*

*First Air Mail from Ireland to England from "Foynes" about 1920*

*Philip Lynch, around 1930*
*Youghal, Cork*

*Auntie Teen, Mick Ahern and Betty*
*Their wedding day I think*

London - about 1935

Annie Condon - who took care of Betty & I in 21, when we were small - forget her? Never! a wonderful person - & loved us.

← Marina Hotel Youghal. Happy times there.

*In the 1930's*

Minnie, Dolly Rogers, & a
Friend - Youghal

Betty in Youghal
about 1938. Appx.

The old Savoy Cinema 1930,
Cork. No longer a Cinema. Good times!

London - Pre-War
about 1937.

Betty - Mick
Aunty Jean
Mick's Car
Youghal
about 1935

Mick had a gas station and car service

Youghal Cork
Betty, Marie Fitzgerald
& Friend - Youghal 193
1935

Dolly Rogers, Betty and Marie Fitzgerald
Youghal

Good friend Bob
Atkins in Youghal
Early Years
He owned the Strand
Palace dance hall

Co. Cork

Youghal 1930's

ABC Cafe 1928

Youghal 1930's

*My Uncle John*

*About 1926*

*Ireland about 1928*

*Youghal, Ireland*

My little cat in 2? Connaught pl Wellington Rd-Cork When I was about 9'

1927
Aunty Teen & friends - Tony Coughlans Model T Ford Youghal 1927.

Co. Cork Ireland 1927

DAD & AUNT TEEN
1920.

1927
Aunty Teen & Aunty (Minnie) (Berlin) on Roof of ABC Cafe Youghal 1927.

*My Aunt Minie's visit to Youghal in 1927 from her home in Berlin, Germany*

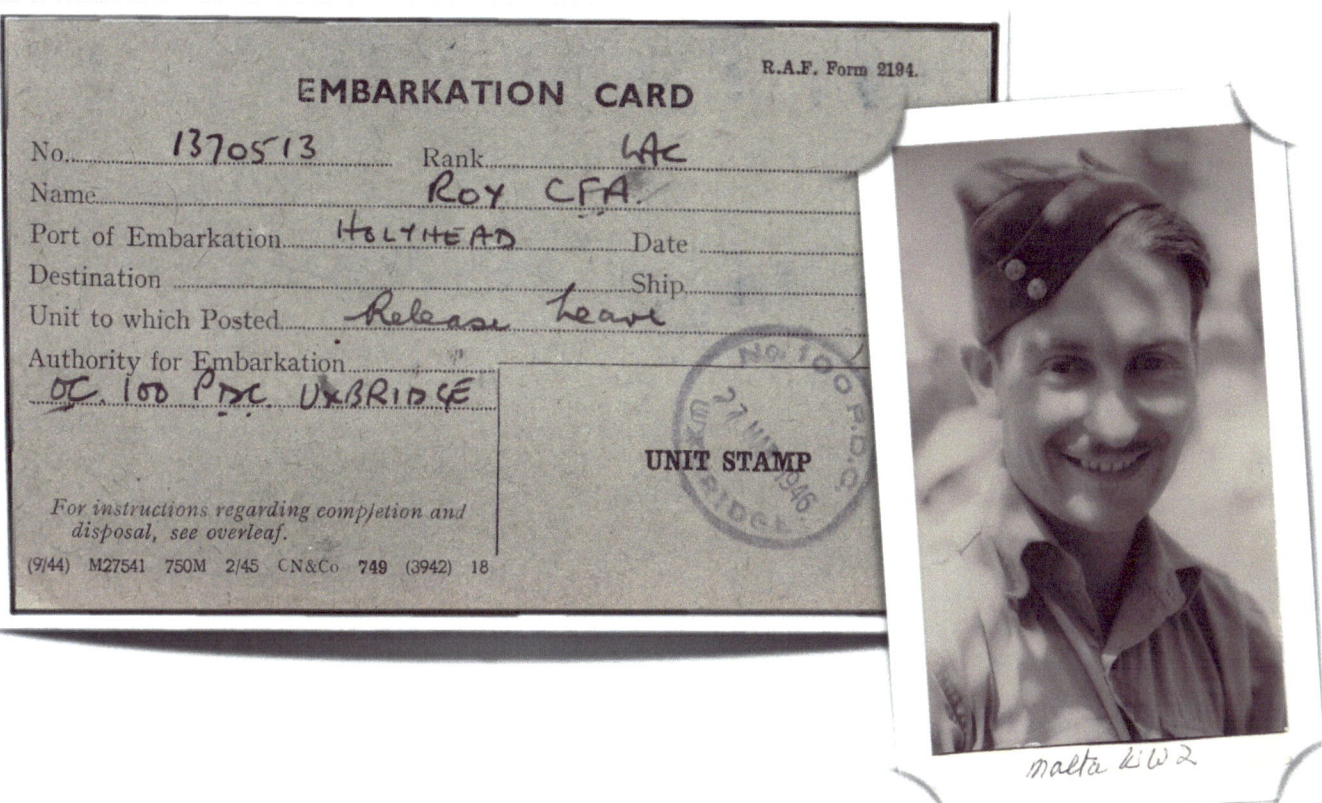

# My Years in the Royal Air Force

Now to my war years and my time in the RAF, Royal Air Force, as a photographer. One of my jobs was to fit the aircraft with cameras to be used to photograph enemy positions. When the planes returned it was our job to develop the film, print pictures, send results to "intelligence", and they in turn would pinpoint enemy targets and the bomber squadrons would then go over and attack the area. I spent three years on "Malta" with some time passing through North Africa. Returning to England and then onto France, when the Germans had moved out and our armies advanced toward Germany. Victory in Europe was celebrated in Paris…quite a time to remember!

The war ends and I go back to England. I get leave to visit Ireland, stayed for a short time with Mime in Dublin, then went to Youghal to visit my sister and husband…Happy times indeed! I intended to go back to England to work there, but fate had other things in store for me.

*First Air Party WW2*
*Before I joined the Royal Air Force*

*During war years and after, the only way to phone my sister Betty was to ring this phone! Outside Betty's home- Youghal*

Captured German Plane. Malta

Chapel of bones! Valetta Malta. War Years. Bombed out!

Bombing on Malta

Bombs on Valletta - Malta

WAR 1939 1945

ARK ROYAL goes down
ARK ROYAL SINKS W.W.2.

Paris - L'Arc de Triomphe
PARIS - LIBERATED - 1945.

Me
V-E. Day Paris!

*Great Day!*

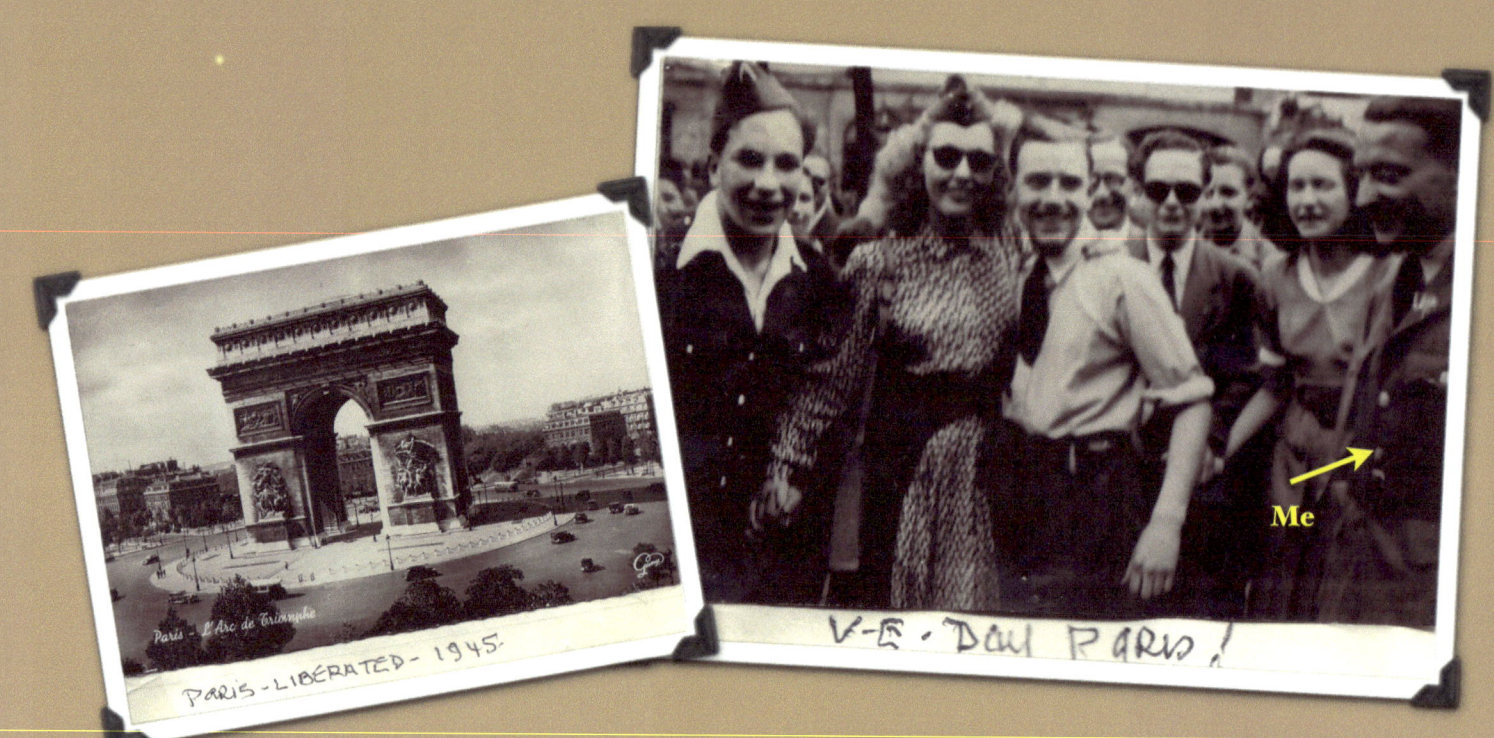

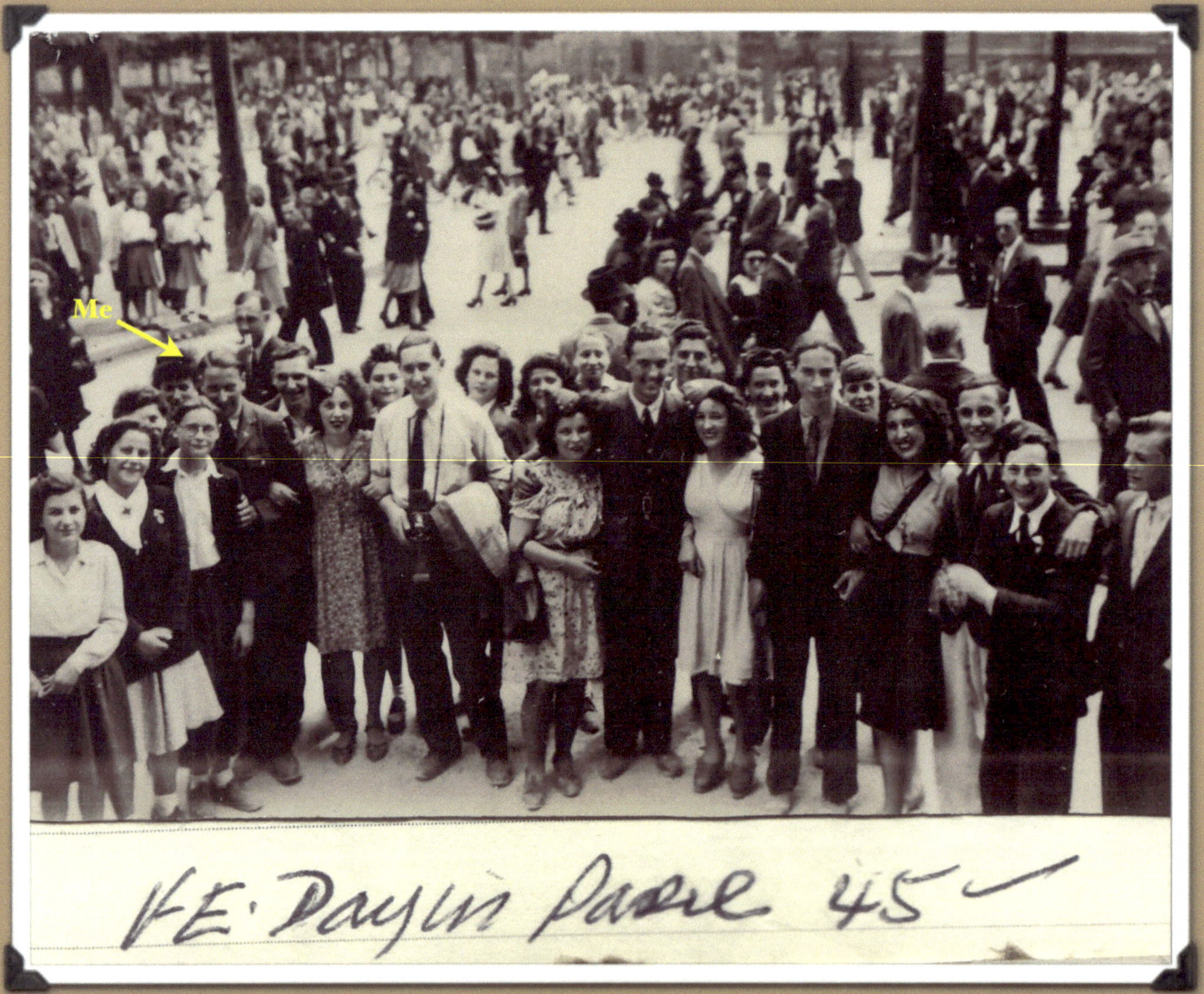
Me
V.E. Day in Paris 45

*Sing me a song! Youghal Co. Cork*

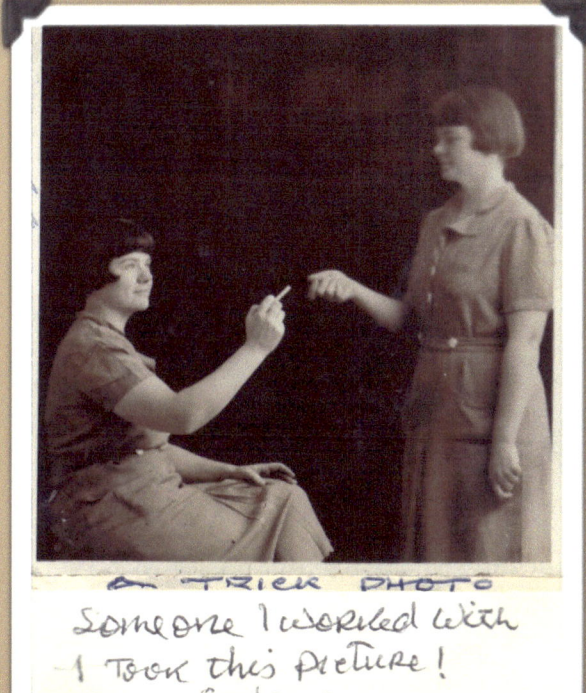

*Trick Picture*

*Nottingham England around 1937*

*Tripoli*

*Rochester Castle*

"Ashton Court" Youghal- Co. CORK. Uncle Bill stayed there, when visiting from the U.S.A.

Tomb of Napoleon Paris

Paris - Panorama des Sept Ponts

*Napoleons Tomb*        *Paris*

one of the last street photographers

Moby Dicks ! Youghal Co CORK

*Moby Dicks Pub. Youghal. Co Cork. Ireland*

*Our Family*
*Me, Kevin, May, Brenda & Richard*

*May - 1947*
*First Home in Youghal, Ireland*

# My Family & Friends

A Mrs. Hennessy from Ballymacode County, Cork, then lived in Youghal, a few doors away from Betty. Her daughters, May, Helen and Kerry, were visiting at the time from the USA. I took May out on a number of dates; we got married October 1st, 1946 in St. Patrick's Church in Cork City!

We rented a bungalow in Youghal and I got a job as a studio photographer in Cork. We were very happy together but May always had a strong urge to return to Boston, where she had lived since her young days. So we went to Boston, living in Broadway, Cambridge.

Our first child was born in St. Elizabeth's Hospital. He gave us great joy. We called him Richard. Then another great happiness came into our lives, a daughter, Brenda, and another son was to come later, Kevin. Our lives were complete.

But still the old feeling of wanting to try Ireland again prompted us to make the trip once more, this time with Richard and Brenda. We bought a nice home on Sleive Rua Drive (Red Mountain), Dublin. The family in Ireland was happy at our return. We had happy times there. But living in Ireland was not to be. After a few years, and some difficult times, we set sail back to Boston, never to return to settle in Ireland. We did go back to visit, many times.

*On the way to Ireland*
*Ship Lacoma*

We bought a house in Winthrop, Mass. Our children went to school there. Richard, Brenda, and Kevin graduated from Winthrop High. Richard married a lovely girl, Maria, from Winthrop. Brenda moved to Newport, RI with her husband, Frank. Kevin moved to Birmingham, Alabama for a number of years and now lives in New Jersey with his wife Kathy.

My dear May passed away a number of years ago. She had not been well for some time. One day she became ill, went to the hospital, about a week later, she held my hand, while I told her I loved her… and the world is never quite the same again.

*About 1935*

*Cambridge, MA*

*Around 1935*

*May, the woman I loved and later married*

*"Seafield" About 1935*

Mrs Hennessy, Helen, Therese, Joan, May - Youghal

Mays Grandmother

Mays Mother and Father
Nora & Richard Hennessy

First home Youghal CO. Cork, Ireland
Seafield 1947

Helen, May Joan - Rug Making - Harvard St Camb.

Helen, May and Joan
Harvard Street, Cambridge, MA

May, years before we met

St. Patricks Church
Cork, Ireland
Where we were Married

Our Wedding Day - 1946 Cork, Ireland

First Married, Youghal - 1947

First Married, Youghal - 1947

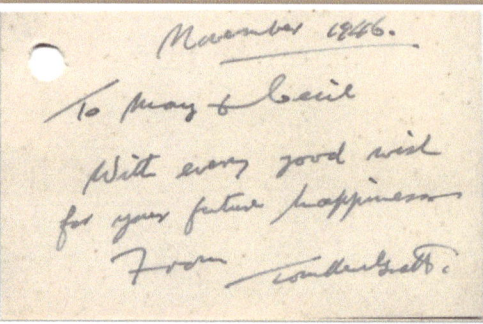

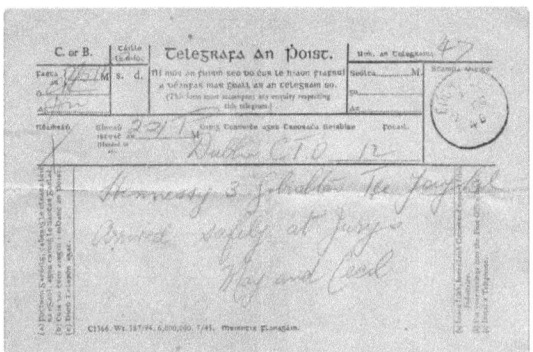
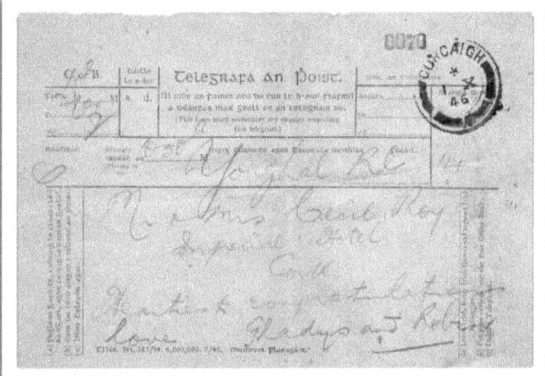
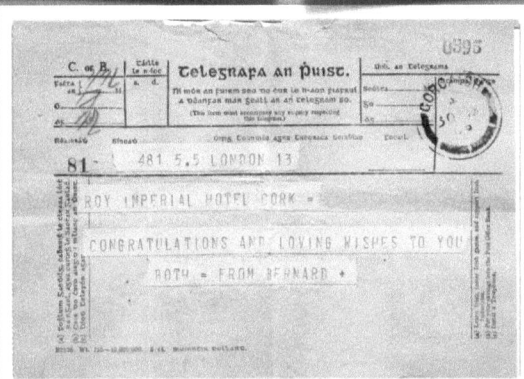
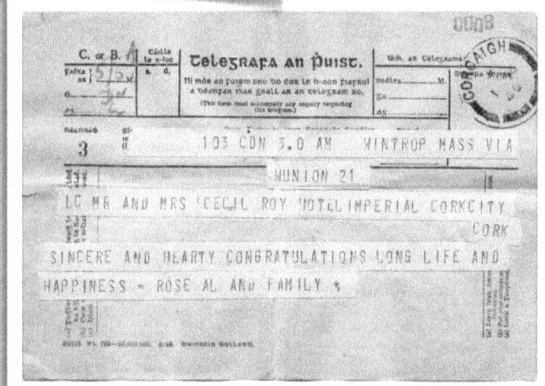
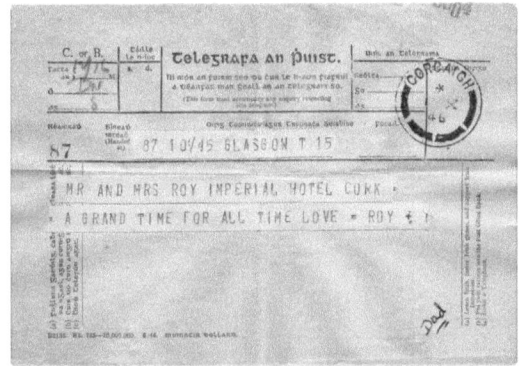
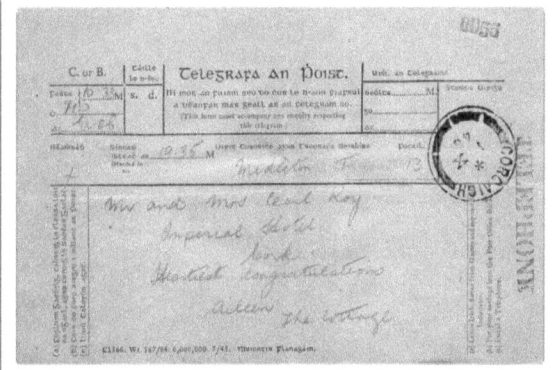
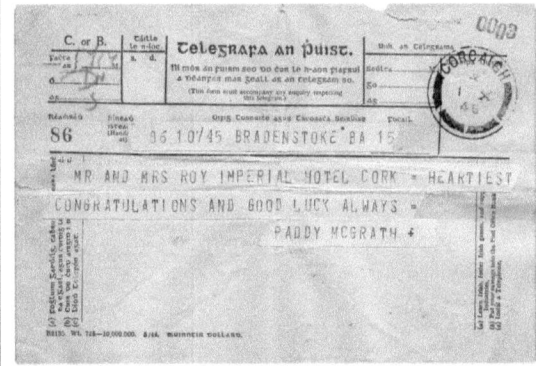
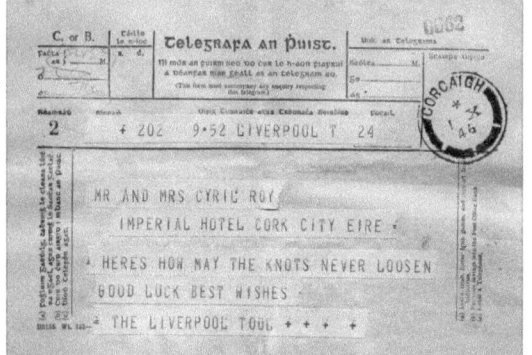
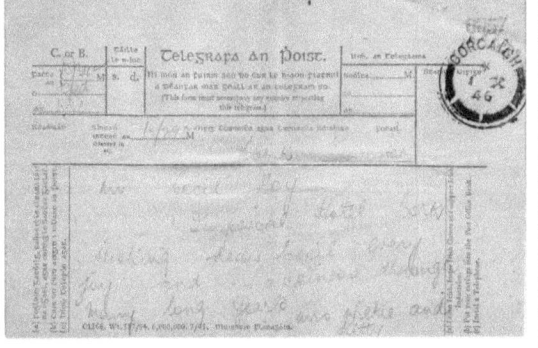
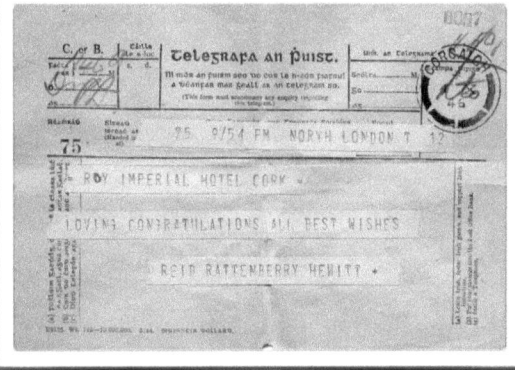

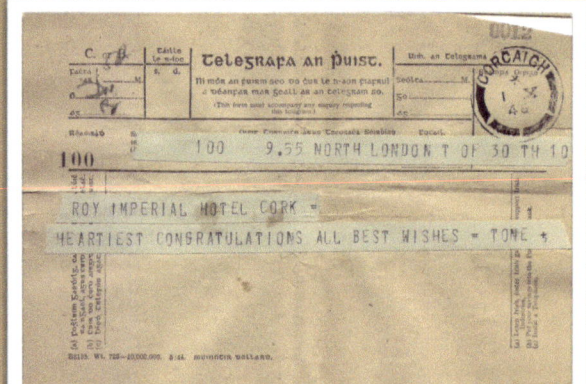
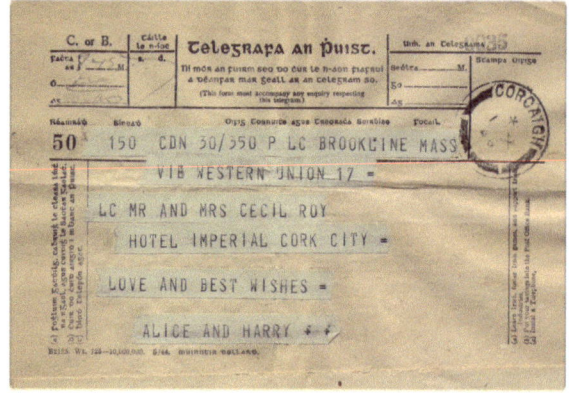
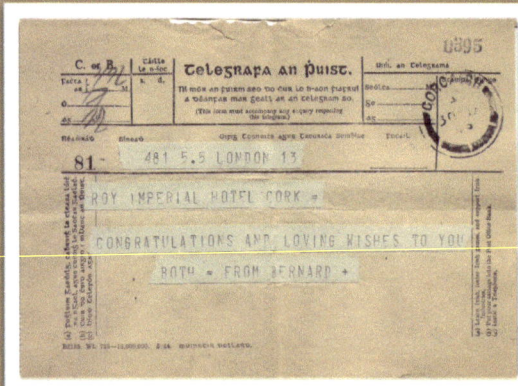
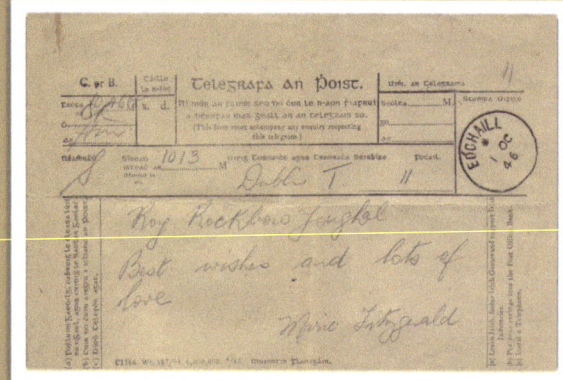
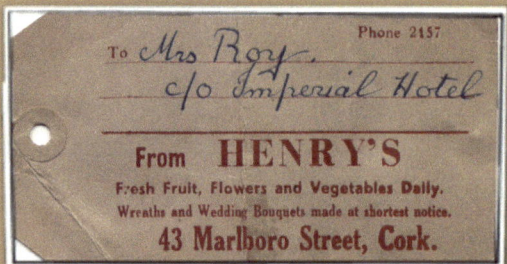

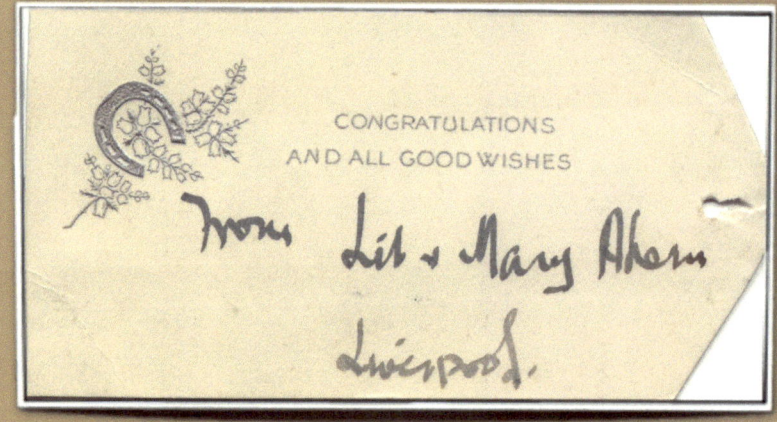

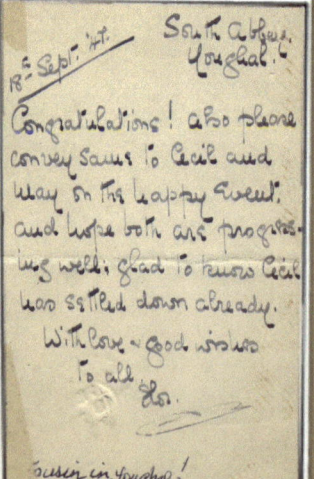
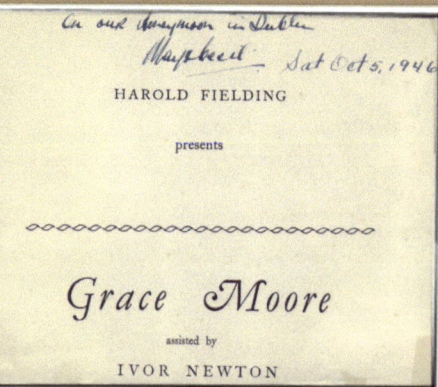

*Show in Dublin, Ireland*
*On our Honeymoon*

Our first home Seafield
Youghal, Co.Cork, Ireland

Our first home Seafield

Around 1952

Christmas, Harvard Street
Cambridge, MA

Around 1947

*Richard, May, Brenda & Kevin*

*May & Richard*
*Harvard Yard, Cambridge, MA*

On Way to Ireland

*Me, Brenda, May & Richard*

Sheil Rua Drive - Stillorgan - Co Dublin

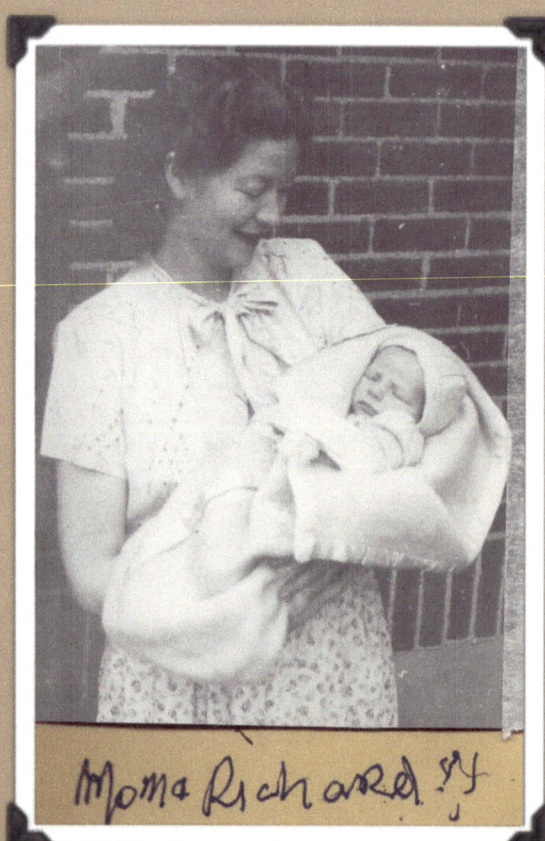

Moma Richard 47

*Around 1947*

*May & Rose*
*Outside Richards Store*

*May & Ricky*

*Mays Sun Flower*

*Mays Garden*
*75 Somerset Ave, Winthrop, MA*

*We miss you Mom*

The Seven Hennessy Sisters
Kerry, Therese, Jule, Rose, Joan, May & Helen

Me, Maria, Steven & May

Marys - Painting

Happy years Later

Moms Garden

Newport RI

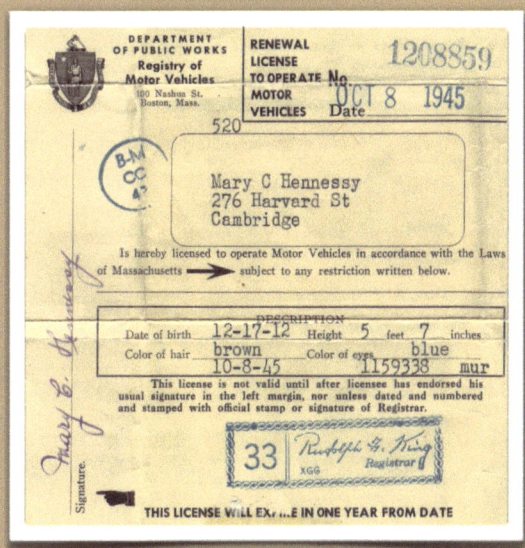

*Linda & John's Wedding*

*Kevin's Graduation*

*75 Somerset Ave, Winthrop, MA*

*Kevin & Marianne's Wedding*

*Rose, Al & Family  
Winhrop, MA*

## My 25th Wedding Anniversary

# MY FAMILY TREE

ALEXANDER
CECIL ROY

MARIANNE
GRIFFIN

KEVIN
ROY

KATHRYN
KASWELL

FRANK
GERARDI

BRENDA
GERARDI

MICHAEL
ROY

ERIN
ROY

KAROLYN
CANONICO

CHRISTENE
GERARDI

RICHARD
GERARDI

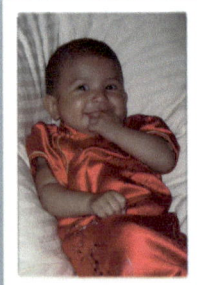

ARIA
GERARDI

**MARY ROY**

**RICHARD ROY**

**MARIA ROY**

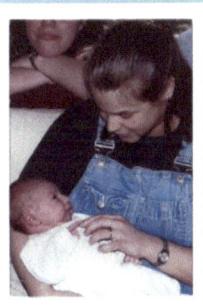
**SAMANTHA COX**

**STEVEN ROY**

**NICHOLAS ROY**

**JEANETTE ROY**

**CHRISTENE GERARDI**

**ALEXANDER COX**

| LEGEND | |
| --- | --- |
| ........ | FORMER RELATION |
| ———— | DIRECT RELATION |

# The Great Blizzard of 1978

## Tall Ships - Boston

Brenda & Richard

Brenda & Richard - Cambridge, MA - 1950

1951

My Family
Frank, Brenda, Kevin, Kathy, Richard, Maria
Nick, Rick, Me, Jeanette - Missing Steven

Brenda First Communion

Brenda & Rick

Newport, RI

Tundra

Simba

Rickey - Mom & Dad

## Brenda's Dolls

Tiffany · Samantha · Lizabeth

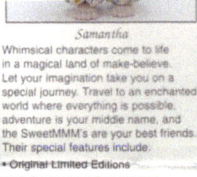

Peter · Margaret

Whimsical characters come to life in a magical land of make-believe. Let your imagination take you on a special journey. Travel to an enchanted world where everything is possible, adventure is your middle name, and the SweetMMM's are your best friends. Their special features include:

- Original Limited Editions
- 15" Quality Vinyl/Fully Jointed
- Hallmarked and Numbered
- Unique Designer Costumes
- Custom Hand Painted Eyes
- Natural Hair Lashes
- Certificate of Authenticity
- Hand Crafted in America
- Guaranteed Smiles

Rosebud · Lili · Missy

Rose · Christina · Emily

Sarah · Michael

### The Christina Doll Collection

The Christina Doll Collection® is a series of Victorian Era dolls stylistic of the grace, elegance and charm of the period. A totally original design by artist, Brenda Elizabeth Gerardi, the collection represents a unique style of opulence and luxury in the world.

Step back in time, to the turn of the century, when the children were dressed in the finest fashions of the day. Beautiful lace trimmed petticoats, bloomers, dresses and bonnets. All of the fashions custom made to perfection with the finest fabrics money could buy.

We have captured and recreated a time gone bye. The Christina Doll Collection® is an Original Limited Edition of only 500 in each design. Their special features include:

- Original Designer Costumes
- German Glass Eyes
- Beautifully Styled Wigs
- Posable Armature Body
- 29" Tall Quality Vinyl
- Special Gift Box
- Signed, Numbered & Hallmarked
- Certificate of Authenticity
- Hand Crafted in America
- Guaranteed Charm & Elegance

☎ 1-800-695-3222

PEGGY MULHOLLAND INC.
NEWPORT, RI 02840

one of Brenda's hand made dolls

Ricky & Grandpa
Newport.

# Alexander The Great (Grandpa)

*Great Grandpa & Alexander Entertaining*

*Great Grandpa & Aria*

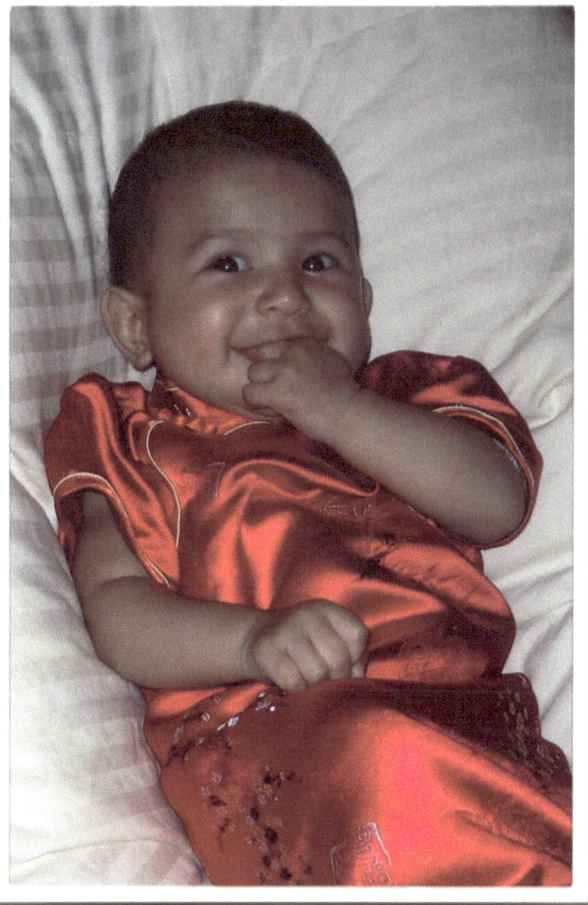

Kathy & Me

# BALLET THEATRE
## OF BOSTON
### José Mateo, Artistic Director

YOUNG DANCERS PROGRAM

YEAR-END
DEMONSTRATION

JUNE 22, 1995

BOSTON CONSERVATORY THEATRE
31 HEMENWAY STREET
BOSTON

## 1994 - 1995 Young Dancers Program

**Pre-Ballet**
Asia Bento
Laura Burleley
Camille Canon
Kayleigh Dudevoir
Barbara Howard
Sabrina Howard
Eva Kielasinski
Diana Kwan
Jessica Lin
James William Lynch Lubkin
Molly Murphy
Stephanie Nunez
Margaret Oliverio
Katerina Stavrianidis
Amandine Ta
Leigh Ward

**LEVEL I**
Tzu-Ying Chuang
Anne Frances Kenney
Ruth Orme-Johnson
Rocio Palomo
Diana Saker
Kathleen Sullivan
Emilia Zambrano

**LEVEL II**
Joylita Bhaskar
Emily Blake
Ashley Bono
Rosa Cao
Danielle Cohen
Michelle Collins
Amelia Fischer
Abigail Friend
Alejandra Hernandez
Gabriella Hernandez
Rebecca Innis
Sadie Jonath
Jenny Lee
Betty Munoz
Alexandra Nassau-Brownstone
Nika Nunley
Orla O'Brien
Maggie Sullivan
Dana Terres
Sarah Trial
Nicole Wehbe
Sasha Wehbe
Shelby Zalewski

**LEVEL III**
Danielle Beaulieu
Allison Bergman
Emily Clark
Kate Collins
Emily Conroy
Andrea Elibero
Lynn Farrugia
Frances Hartmann
Abigail Hemnes
Alexandra Irving
Joanne Kim
Jessica Lambert
Elizabeth Manganiello
David Ricker
Sarah Rogge
Francy Rontayne
Wendy Shinzawa
Vera Vine
Alexandra Zaltman

**LEVEL IV**
Megan Crotty
Lesley Anne Day
Christine De Salvo
Melissa Gelfand
Amy Hughes
Laurel Kaan
Nahede Khosrovi
Emily Mantz
Carolyn Paine
Amy Pradell
Erin Roy
Alison Waggener

**LEVEL V**
Alyssa Bullard
Sarah Case
Jessica Cheney
Caroline Donchess
Natalie Lambert
Erin Martin
Kristin Sloan
Katerina Turner

**LEVEL VI**
Amanda Beavers
Micha Burns
Tiffany Ely
Elizabeth Scherban

**INSTRUCTORS**
**PRE-BALLET**
Marisa Solis

**LEVEL I**
Rebecca Arnold

**LEVEL II**
Rebecca Arnold
Marisa Solis

**LEVEL III**
Merryn Frazer
Jose Mateo

**LEVEL IV**
Rebecca Arnold
Todd Hall

**LEVEL V-VI**
Todd Hall
Jose Mateo
Mary McKenzie Thompson

**PIANISTS**
Kevin Galie
Rosalie Hoffman-Goumas
Michael Katzman
Stephen LaRoche
Angelo Mammano
Jeanne McKenzie
Richard Pinnell
Slava Samandorov
Alla Troyanovsky

Erin

Michael - School - Birmingham - AL

to Granpa
From Mike
Love

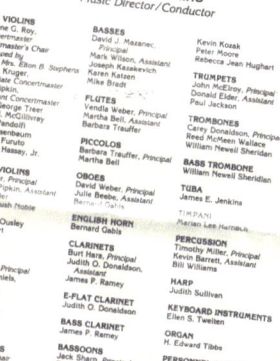

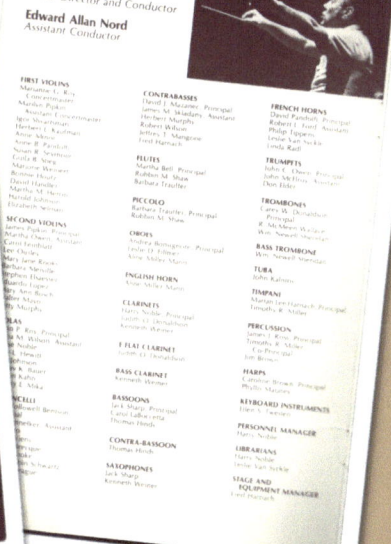

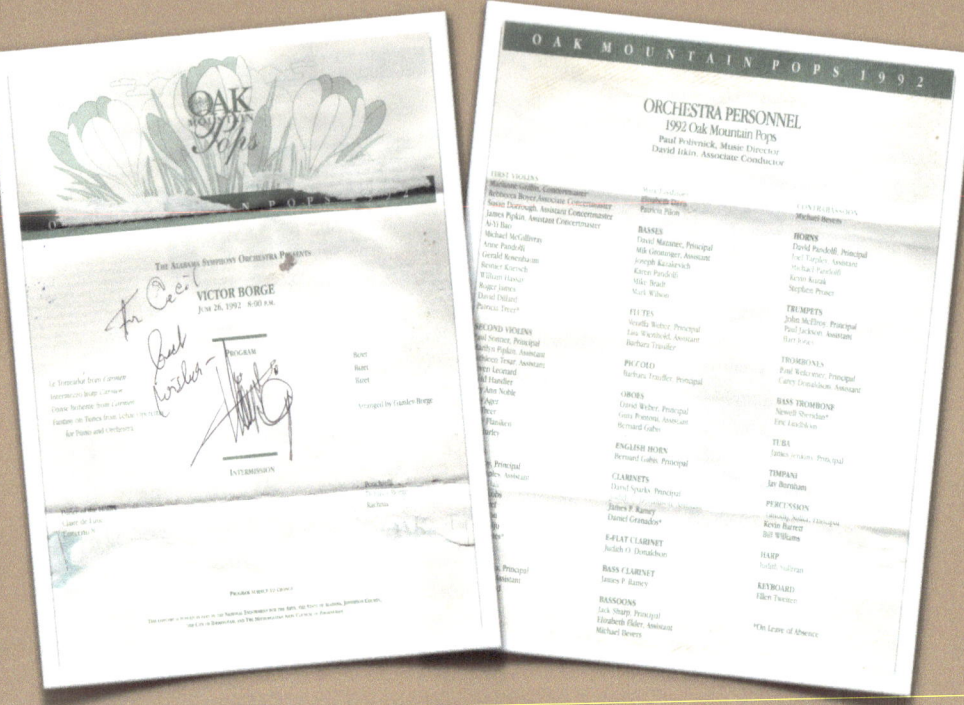

## ALABAMA SYMPHONY ORCHESTRA

### PROGRAM

Paul Polivnick, Music Director ■ David Itkin, Associate Conductor

DECEMBER 8, 1991, 3:00 pm

### MITCH MILLER

| | |
|---|---|
| Deck the Halls | Hershey Kay |
| Hallelujah Chorus from Messiah | George Frideric Handel |
| Fantasia on Greensleeves | Ralph Vaughan Williams |
| Jesu, Joy of Man's Desiring | Johann Sebastian Bach |
| March of the Toys from Babes in Toyland | Victor Herbert |
| The Wizard of Oz | Arlen-Harburg |

### INTERMISSION

| | |
|---|---|
| Sleigh Ride | Leroy Anderson |
| Fum, Fum, Fum | Arr. by Robert Shaw |
| Carol of the Drums | Arr. by Davis |
| Carol of the Bells | M. Leontovich, Arr. by Peter Wilhousky |
| A Christmas Carol Sing-A-Long | |
| White Christmas | Irving Berlin |

Memories

HARVARD ST - Cambridge

## Winthrop Sailor Gets Unit Citation

GREAT LAKES, Ill. (FHT-NC)—Seaman Recruit Richard M. Roy, USN, 20, son of Mr. and Mrs. Alexander C. Roy of 76 Somerset Ave., Winthrop, has been graduated from nine weeks of Navy basic training at the Naval Training Center here.

In the first weeks of his naval service he studied military subjects and lived and worked under conditions similar to those he will encounter on his first ship or at his first shore station.

Richard - Navy days

Better-Buy - opening day

Richard in HARVARD St Camb.

Richard Kevin & Brenda HARVARD St Camb MA.

Richard

Playdoe

Mitze

Mitze

Aidan & Betty

Moira & Bill Wedding Day - 1960

The Whole Gang
At Rose and Al's home in Winthrop, MA

Maureen, Me & Carol

The Sales Family
Children of Barry and Jule Sales

Dorathy & Maureen

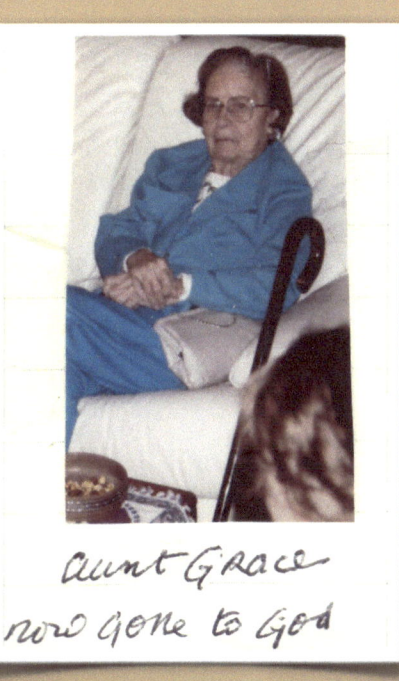

Bill Parkers Aunt

My Birthday - Maureen's home in Quincy, MA

Sheila OBrian and Me
Quincy, MA
A very good freind

Mays sisters Joan & Helen
with a friend and I
Youghal, Ireland

Buskers Pub, Newport, RI

Dougie and I
My friend Bill Askews brother in law
Barrow, England 1995

Good friends of my young days in Youghal
Co. Cork, Ireland Around 1935

- the family -

Sean & Kevin - Cambridge, MA

Richard's Birthday

Paddy Mcgrath & Family

Me, Dot & John Okeefe

Hilda & Aidan - Wedding Day Around 1970

Wedding of Dot Okeefes daughter

Aidan and Hildas Wedding - Around 1970

Brendan & Therese

Mr. & Mrs. David Parker

Paddy & Kerrys daughters Ann and Jan McGrath

Dublin, Ireland

Therese Fallon
Dublin, Ireland

*Justin & Joan - Trophy - "Mr What" Grand National Winner - Recent visit to Ireland.*

*A good friend Nancy - Newport, RI*

*Therese with her Dad Leonard Walsh*

Therese with her dad Leonard Walsh

*May Bayerinsky. Weihnachten 1918. Xmas - holidays 1917 taken in the country.*

Cousin Mays visit to Cork from Germany

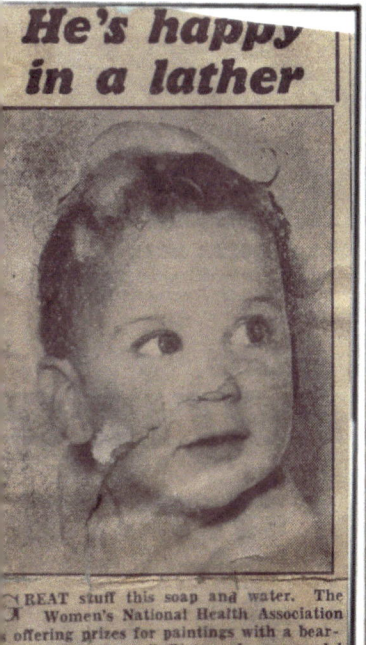

Kevin Roy

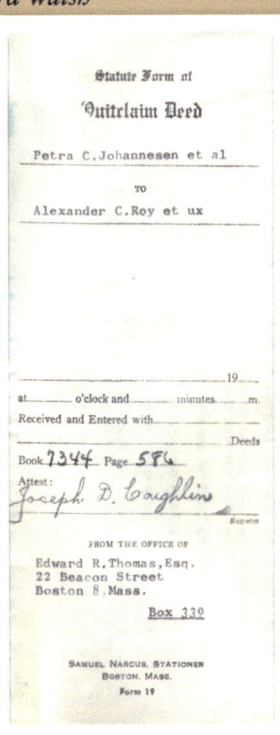

Deed from 75 Somerset Ave Winthrop, MA

A good friend Nancy - Newport, RI

*Some Currency from my Travels*

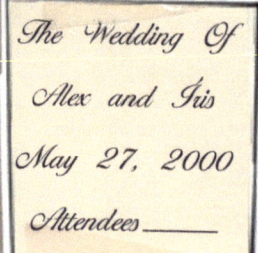

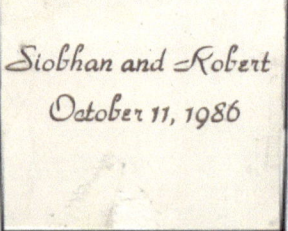
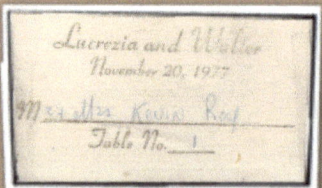

# Thacher School

In June of 1971 Cecil's cousin Maureen decided to open her own Montessori school. She made it a non-profit organization, invited Cecil to be on the board of Trustees and set out in search of a location. This search took all of June and July and finally on August 28th a lease was signed for a room in the Thacher Building in Milton. The place was a mess. A real mess. In fact the building was taken off the condemned list in order to rent it to us. It took eighteen gallons of paint to make it look even passably presentable. Cecil was a trump. He did all the detailed work...the window frames were the worst and Cec took care of all of them. The school opened in mid September with sixteen children and in two years had outgrown the space. We moved to Curry College and from there to a closed public school in Milton. By now there were almost 200 children enrolled.

As the school's needs grew it became evident that we should build our own building. Cecil took charge of the photography for the fundraising brochure. He came to the school and took some candid shots as well as staged ones. There was one special picture, which we all loved and he still talks about. He also made a Celtic design plaque, which to this day hangs in the foyer of the school.

In 1987 we bought land and in 1989 we built an 11,000 sq. ft. school. We had six classrooms, a library, a multi purpose room, a staff lounge and offices. In 1991 we added an additional classroom and in 1994 we built a gym, an art room, a science room, some offices and we enlarged two classrooms. Although by now Cec was no longer on the Board he was always there in spirit, always asking about the school and always remembering those "early years".

This year the school has added a second story...more classrooms, a second activity center, a conservatory, a kitchen, a tutorial room, and two more offices. I look forward to taking Cecil up to see it when it is finished. He will be so proud to see that what he was such an integral part of is such a successful school.

Of course Maureen has also long since retired and on that day Cecil presented her with a poem in honor of the occasion. She keeps in framed in her living room.

**Founders Cecil Roy, Maureen Coughlan, Head of Thacher, Sheila O'Brien and a founding parent, Linda Badoian break the first ground for Thacher's new "addition" at the BIG DIG on February 13th.**

ABSENT FOUNDER MOIRA PORTER

Past Pupil / my photo / Thacher

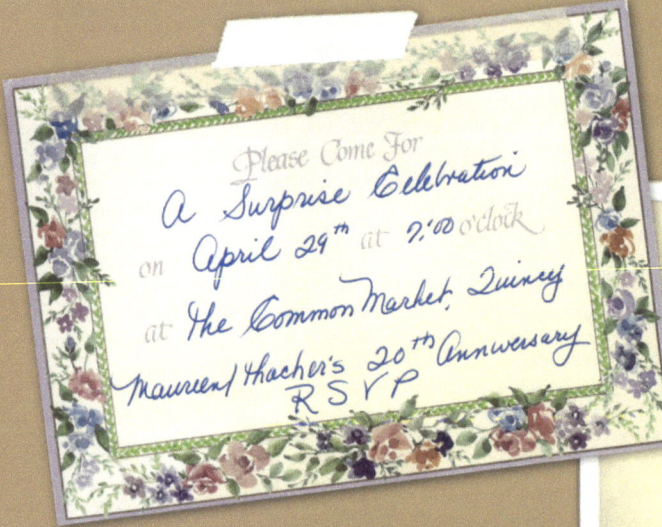

Please Come For
A Surprise Celebration
on April 29th at 7:00 o'clock
at The Common Market, Quincy
Maureen Thacher's 20th Anniversary
RSVP

You are proudly invited to our gala
OPEN HOUSE
to celebrate the opening of
THACHER MONTESSORI SCHOOL'S
New Building
on
Sunday, September 10, 1989
from 1:00-3:00 pm
at 1425 Blue Hill Avenue, Milton, MA

Please join us on this special occasion!

To Maureen – the year 1997
Your Retirement from Thatcher Montessori School

The Story in my book of life in nearing its completion.
What Love I gave comes back to me, my cup is filled full measure.
And as the pages slip away, and there is time for me to say
How much your Love I treasure.

Proud of you I am and all you've done – surmounting obstacles one by one
Through many years to see you Thatcher dream come true.
How many memories must fill your mind of children's faces left behind
And now as adults grow
And still they come like the first child came to Thatcher
When you started long ago.

Your School will live in memory of your dream that did come true.
And of countless little children and their special love for you.
The name of Maureen Coughlan will be forever in their mind,
Long after their childhood days and the School they left behind.

Long live Thatcher Montessori School, its foundress and friend.
God bless the School she started. God be with it to the end.

With Love,
Cecil Roy – July 1997

Dear Mrs. Ross —

The photo you sent brought back so many memories of Dublin and the time we spent there — and, of course, dear Rock — we miss him so much — Thank you so very much — I do hope you will have a chance to see our play — I think you would enjoy it. So — Top of the morning and the rest of the day! — the old Irish greeting —

Thank you again —

Barbara Rush

**STEEL MAGNOLIAS** Six women, four of them habitues of a tacky beauty salon in Louisiana, share their trials and tribulations in this acclaimed comedy by Robert Harling. The national touring version has opened at the newly renovated Wilbur Theater. 3 p.m. 246 Tremont St. Telephone (617) 426-9366. Tickets $25-$37.50. Play runs through Oct. 22.

WILBUR THEATRE — BOSTON
Owned and operated by New Wilbur Theatre, Inc.
Myrna Merowitz, President

ELLIOT MARTIN  MICHAEL FRAZIER  JAMES M. NEDERLANDER
present

**BARBARA RUSH   MARION ROSS
CAROLE COOK**  1989

in

*Steel Magnolias*

by
ROBERT HARLING

also starring

MARGO MARTINDALE   TRACY SHAFFER   DAWN HOPPER

Scenery by            Lighting by           Costumes by
EDWARD T. GIANFRANCESCO  MARTIN ARONSTEIN   GARLAND RIDDLE

Hair Design & Supervision        Production Stage Manager
BOBBY H. GRAYSON                 ELLIOTT WOODRUFF

Casting by                General Manager
MARJORIE MARTIN           CHARLOTTE WILCOX

Directed by
PAMELA BERLIN

Originally produced on the New York Stage by
the WPA Theatre (Kyle Renick, Artistic Director)

Presented in Boston by

Dublin Ireland & Rock Hudson Barbara Rush About 1942!

Rock Hudson - Barbara Rush Dublin 1947? - 48 -

King of England
England's King - Malta 1943

DUBLIN IRELAND PRESIDENT TRUEMAN AND PARTY.
presidents daughter on right

John Huston Gregory Peck "Moby Dick" Youghal

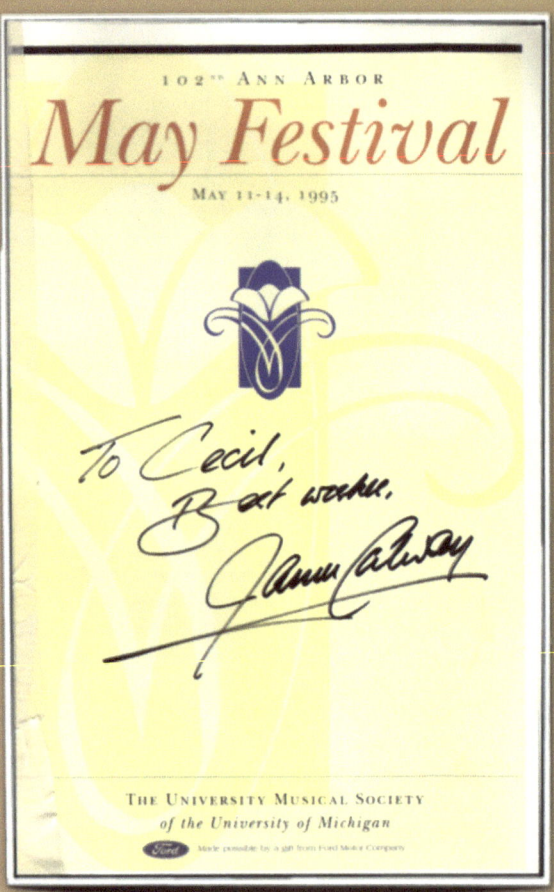

President Kennedy's funeral

# People now gone that were important to me

*The Family of the late*
*Tom and Margaret McGrath*
*thank you most sincerely for your kind*
*expression of sympathy in their*
*recent bereavements.*

*The Holy Sacrifice of the Mass has been*
*offered for your intentions.*

"Roseville", Cahir, Co. Tipperary.

---

**MERKLE**—Of Belmont, January 16, Helen M. (Hennessy), mother of Joan, Ellen and Charles Merkle; sister of Mrs. Cecil Roy (May), Mrs. Albert Mahegan (Rose), both of Winthrop, Mrs. Patrick A. McGrath (Kerry) of Belmont, and Mrs. James (Joan) Kennedy, Thomas and Maurice Hennessy, all of Ireland. Funeral from the Short, Williamson & Diamond Funeral Home, 52 Trapelo Rd., BELMONT, Tuesday, January 18 at 8 a.m. Funeral Mass in St. Joseph's Church, Common St., Belmont at 9 o'clock. Friends may call at the funeral home Monday 2-4 and 7-9 p.m.

---

**John Fitzgerald Kennedy**
35th President of the United States
Born May 29, 1917
Inaugurated January 20, 1961
Died November 22, 1963

---

℞

*Maurice Hennessy*

*Aileen, the boys and Aileen*
*deeply appreciate and will always hold in grateful*
*remembrance your kind expression of sympathy*
*with them at the time of our sad bereavement.*

*The Holy Sacrifice of the Mass will be*
*offered for your intentions.*

The Rectory Lodge,
Mogeely,
Co. Cork.     April, 1996.

---

**MAHEGAN**—Of Winthrop August 13, Albert C.J. Mahegan age 78. Beloved husband of the late Rose (Hennessy). Father of Jule Sales of FL, Albert Mahegan of Westwood, Kerry Melanson of Burlington, Susan DeFelice of Swampscott, Linda Cramer of Winthrop, Robert Mahegan of Marblehead, Donald Mahegan of Danvers, Siobhan Dalton of NH, Maureen Mahegan of Winthrop and David Mahegan of FL. Dear brother of the late Kathryn McNeeley. Also survived by 21 grandchildren and 2 great-grandchildren. Funeral from the Maurice W. Kirby Funeral Home, 210 Winthrop St., WINTHROP Saturday at 9:15. Funeral Mass in The Church of St. John The Evangelist at 10. Relatives and friends invited. Former Buick salesman for 35 years, life member Cottage Park Yacht Club, former member of Board of Finance Winthrop Savings Bank, former member Board of Trustees Winthrop Community Hospital and late Navy veteran W.W. II. In lieu of flowers, expressions of sympathy in Albert's name may be made to Winthrop Association of Retarded Citizens, 63 Atlantic St., Winthrop, MA 02152. Interment Winthrop Cemetery. Visiting hours Friday evening only 7-9.

---

## AHERN

MY Very sincere, heartfelt thanks to all my relations and friends for the expression of their sorrow at the death of my dearest sister, Betty Ahern, of Youghal, Co. Cork. I will remember you all with kindness" and in my prayers and wish you all every blessing from the Lord.
—Cecil Roy.

---

**Five Year**
**Certificate of Associate Membership**
FOR

Mary C. Roy

Deceased Members Share in
2500 Masses offered each year
Solemn Requiem High Mass and nine
Novenas of Masses each November
Daily public prayers offered in all our
Seminaries and Mission Houses

**Enrolled by**

Bill and Moira Parker

COLUMBAN  FATHERS

MILTON, MASS.

---

## Gerardo Gerardi
## September 15, 1980

Do not let your hearts be troubled.

Trust In God still, and trust In me.

There are many rooms In my
   fathers house;

If there were not, I should have
   told you.

I am going now to prepare a place for

you, and after I have gone and prepared

you a place, I shall return to take you

with me; So, that where I am you may

be too.

JOHN 14 (vs. 1-3)

*Memorial & Hambly*
*Funeral Homes*
*Newport, Rhode Island*

---

*The family of the late*
*Sheila O'Brien*
*thank you most sincerely for your kind*
*expression of sympathy in their*
*recent bereavement.*
*The Holy Sacrifice of the Mass will be*
*offered for your intentions.*

3, Vernon Grove,
Rathgar,
Dublin 6.     September, 1997.

*In Remembrance!*

Sacred Heart of Jesus, I place my trust in Thee.

✠

PRAY FOR THE SOUL OF

**Dorothy Forster Prior Watson**

Merville, Youghal, Co. Cork, who died on 30TH. APRIL, 1960

R.I.P.

I heard a voice from heaven saying to me—Blessed are the dead that die in the Lord. From henceforth now, saith the Spirit, that they rest from their labours for their works follow them.
(Apocalypse of St. John, c. 14)

Monaloe Stationery, 14 Hawkins St., Dublin

---

"We never lose those we give to God."        St. Augustine

✝

IN LOVING MEMORY OF

**Kathryn J. McNeeley**

March 8, 1996

May you always walk in sunshine and God's love around you flow, for the happiness you gave us, no one will ever know.

---

We, Maureen and Justin thank you most sincerely for your kind expression of sympathy on the recent death of our dear brother

*Alfred Coughlan*

The Holy Sacrifice of the Mass has been offered for your intentions.

"Deelish,"
King Edward Road,
Bray.                    September, 199

---

In Memory of
**Julia A. Magni**
Died: Oct. 7, 1970

Deliver us, Lord, from every evil,
and grant us peace in our day,
In your mercy keep us free from sin
and protect us from all anxiety
as we wait in joyful hope
for the coming of our Savior, Jesus Christ.

**REILEY FUNERAL HOME**

SALVATION SERIES          PRINTED IN ITALY

*Mom's Sister - Aunt Jule*

---

SACRED HEART OF JESUS
have mercy on the soul of
**Christy Fallon**
Phibsboro, Dublin
who died
on the 5th May, 1997
Aged 84 Years
R.I.P.

Fold him, O Jesus, in Thy arms,
And let him henceforth be,
A messenger of love between
Our human hearts and thee.

---

"We never lose those we give to God."        St. Augustine

In Loving Memory of
**Francis P. Gilfoyle**
November 30, 1982

May you always walk in sunshine and God's love around you flow, for the happiness you gave us, no one will ever know. It broke our hearts to lose you, but you did not go alone, a part of us went with you, the day God called you home. A million times we've needed you. A million times we've cried. If love could only have saved you. You never would have died.

The Lord be with you
And May You Rest in Peace. Amen.

*My friend from the Cottage Jackie*

BRENDAN'S FATHER →

---

"My Aunt Teen"

✝

**Pray For**
THE REPOSE OF THE SOUL OF
**DORATHEA O'RIORDAN**
Who died 9th March, 1959
R.I.P.

✠

O GENTLEST Heart of Jesus, ever present in the Blessed Sacrament, ever consumed with burning love for the poor captive souls in Purgatory, have mercy on the soul of Thy servant, DORATHEA; bring her from the shadows of exile to Thy bright home in Heaven, where, we trust Thou and Thy Blessed Mother have woven for her a crown of unfading bliss. Amen.

Jesus, Mary and Joseph, I give you my heart and my soul.

Jesus, Mary and Joseph, assist me now and in my last agony.

Jesus, Mary and Joseph, may I breathe forth my soul in peace with you. Amen.—7 years and 7 quarantines.

Editions de la Grande Trappe - Orne

---

✝

In Loving Memory of
**JOHN J. O'KEEFE**
1912 - 1991

The Lord is my Shepherd; I shall not want. In verdant pastures He gives me repose; before restful waters He leads me; He refreshes my soul. He guides me in right paths for His name's sake. Even though I walk in the dark valley I fear no evil; for You are at my side With Your rod and Your staff that give me courage. You spread a table for me in the sight of my foes; You anoint my head with oil; my cup overflows. Only goodness and kindness follow me all the days of my life; and I shall dwell in the house of the Lord for years to come.

---

We, Maureen and Justin thank you most sincerely for your kind expression of sympathy on the recent death of our dear brother

*Alfred Coughlan*

The Holy Sacrifice of the Mass has been offered for your intentions.

"Deelish,"
King Edward Road,
Bray.                    September

Sacred Heart of Jesus, I place my trust in Thee.

✠

PRAY FOR THE SOUL
OF
Dorothy Forster
Prior Watson
Merville, Youghal, Co. Cork,
who died on
30TH. APRIL, 1960

R. I. P.

I heard a voice from heaven saying to me—Blessed are the dead that die in the Lord. From henceforth now, saith the Spirit, that they rest from their labours for their works follow them.
(Apocalypse of St. John, c. 14)

Monaloe Stationery, 14 Hawkins St., Dublin

---

"We never lose those we give to God."       St. Augustine

IN LOVING MEMORY OF
Kathryn J. McNeeley
March 8, 1996

May you always walk in sunshine and God's love around you flow, for the happiness you gave us, no one will ever know.

---

We, Maureen and Justin
thank you most sincerely for your kind
expression of sympathy on the recent death
of our dear brother
Alfred Coughlan
The Holy Sacrifice of the Mass has been
offered for your intentions.

"Deelish,"
King Edward Road,
Bray.                                September, 199

---

DOUG HICKTON
Nicest man you
could meet

# Ex-AFC star's funeral today

---

It is in dying that we are born into eternal life.
St. Francis of Assisi

IN LOVING MEMORY OF
ANTONETTA T. BENINATI
Died November 16, 1982

Perhaps you sent a lovely card,
Or sat quietly in a chair;
Perhaps you sent a floral piece,
If so, we saw it there.

Perhaps you spoke the kindest words,
As any friend could say;
Perhaps you were not there at all,
Just thought of us that day.

Whatever you did to console our hearts,
We thank you so much whatever the part

---

In Loving Memory
— of —
Mary Hackett
Tallow Street, Youghal,
Co. Cork.
Who died on
4th June, 1996.
Aged 76 years.
Rest in Peace.

Mother of my friend - Mike Hackett

---

One of Dear Moms
Old Best Friends

Jesus, Mercy    Mary, Help

✠

OF YOUR CHARITY
Pray for the repose of the Soul of
CLEMENT WATSON
Merville, Youghal, Co. Cork
Who died on 25th November, 1968
AGED 80 YEARS

R. I. P.

✠

Eternal Rest grant unto him, O Lord.
Sacred Heart of Jesus, I place all my trust in Thee.

Field, Youghal.

---

IN LOVING MEMORY OF
THE AHERNE - FAMILY
THE STRAND
BRIDGET, MICHAEL,
NORA, JACK, MARY,
NANCY & EILEEN
ELIZABETH NEE ROY
R.I.P.

---

IN LOVING MEMORY OF
JOHN J. TATTAN
November 2, 1982

Your gentle face and patient smile
With sadness we recall
You had a kindly word for each
And died beloved by all.
The voice is mute and stilled the heart
That loved us well and true.
Ah, bitter was the trial to part
From one so good as you.
You are not forgotten loved one
Nor will you ever be
As long as life and memory last
We will remember thee.
We miss you now, our hearts are sore,
As time goes by we miss you more,
Your loving smile, your gentle face
No one can fill your vacant place.

Friend of our Family

# Some of my Poems

## LADY THROUGH A WINDOW

One day while walking in the rain
I chanced to see a lovely lady
Looking through her window pane

She smiled at me as I passed by,
Her smile lit up the darkened clouds
And the sun came out from a clear blue sky.

The lady smiled again at me
As I turned to wave good-bye.

## TO BABY CHLOE

A pretty face to light your day,
Two little arms outstretched as if to say
I love you Mom and Dad, I'm here to stay.
Two little legs whose rhythm seems to play
Imaginary happy tunes on soft white pillows day by day.
A cry that makes you know when hunger is near,
A smile that makes the darkest day seem bright and clear.
This joy, this blessing from above
Given to you both to hold and love.
Oh! How could any gift replace
The happy smile upon your baby's face.

To Maureen - the year 1997
Your Retirement from Thatcher Montessori School

The Story in my book of life in nearing its completion,
What Love I gave comes back to me, my cup is filled full measure,
And as the pages slip away, and there is time for me to say
How much your Love I treasure.

Proud of you I am and all you've done - surmounting obstacles one by one
Through many years to see your Thatcher dream come true.
How many memories must fill your mind of children's faces left behind
And now as adults grow
And still they come like the first child came to Thatcher
When you started long ago.

Your School will live in memory of your dream that did come true,
And of countless little children and their special love for you.
The name of Maureen Coughlan will be forever in their mind,
Long after their childhood days and the School they left behind.

Long live Thatcher Montessori School, its foundress and friend,
God bless the School she started, God be with it to the end.

With Love,
Cecil Roy - July 1977


## TWO SWANS ON A LAKE – BETTY AHERN

Two swans on a lake in graceful perfection,
Morn's golden sky in glacial reflection.
A moment of beauty clearly defined,
Caught for all time in the web of the mind.

## THE OLD PIANO IN 21 CONNAUGHT PLACE, CORK – LONG AGO

When as a child, a few years old,
My mother sang to me, I'm told,
A lullaby, on this piano,
Friend of mine.

It is old in years, this piano, I remember well,
If it could speak, what happy moments it could tell,
Of music played upon its ivory keys,
Of songs we loved to sing in days gone by,
My family and I.

For you have served us well
Some loved ones gone.
Play on this old piano, friend of mine,
For music and for song,
For you will play till all your notes are gone.

Play on for families to come,
Play on old friend of mine,
Play on.

2000

## THE COTTAGE ON THE HILL

As I walked along the country road
And had some time to kill
I took a look at that old cottage,
That old cottage on the hill.

Who once lived there ? what would I find ?
How many thoughts had filled my mind.
Were children playing where now the tall weeds stand,
Were many clothes upon the line,
Now broken by the winter's clime,
Or just two old folks living out their time.
The shutters on the windows swinging to and fro,
That once gave them protection from the storms of long ago.

I pause a little longer with a prayer or two in mind
For the people in that cottage and the times they left behind.
Oh what memories could unfold if broken walls could speak
And tales be told.

## SO LITTLE TIME THE OLD MAN SAID

So little time when morning dawns
To watch the shadows on the grass,
As sun breaks through the darkened sky of night.

So little time is left to hear the young birds call,
Or watch the robin on the wing,
To listen to his song as winter turns to spring.
The fleeting hours of time go by,
Summer replaces spring,
Roses grow and little daisies push their tiny heads
Out of the vast wilderness of the green grass.

So little time when autumn comes,
To see again God's art, painting the
Landscape with color, such beauty to behold,
So soon to fade as winter cold arrives
And snow-packed mountains
Reach the sky, and darkened clouds prevail.

So little time is left to watch the young folks play,
To hear a baby cry at the miracle of birth,
And watch them grow from day to day.

To offer a hand in friendship
And have it returned in kind.
To have your loved ones near,
Or even in a distant land,
Where loving ties remain within the mind.

So little time to say again I care,
And hold your loved ones near.

I say to you who still retain your youth,
You too will grow old like me.
But mark it well! Be loving while you can,
Be kind while you can.
Be a friend to those in need, and
Take the time to watch the flowers grow.

For youth grows old too fast I fear,
Take this advice from me! I know.

## LASKA

*(This is the story of an old gentleman relating to his friends in a men's club in England, the story of his love for a beautiful girl that still remains with him through the years. His love – Laska, the place – down by the Rio Grande)*

It's all very well to write reviews, to carry umbrellas and to wear dry shoes,
To say what everyone is saying here, and to wear what everyone else must wear,
But to night I'm sick of the whole affair, I want free life and I want fresh air,
I sigh for the canter after the cattle, the crack of the whips like shots in battle,
The melee of horns of hoofs and heads that wars, wrangles, scatters and spreads,
For the green beneath and the blue above, for dash and danger, life and love,
And "Laska"

Laska used to ride on a mouse grey mustang close by my side,
With green serape and bright bell spur, I laughed with joy as I looked at her,
She was as bold as the billows that beat, as brave as the breezes that blow from her little head
 to her little feet,

She was swayed in her suppleness too and fro by each just of passion.
The sapling pine that grows at the end of the Kansas bluff,
And wars with the wind when the weather is rough
Is like this Laska, this love of mine.

She would hunger that I might eat, take the bitter and leave me the sweet,
But one night as I made her jealous for fun, something I'd said or something I'd done,
One night in San Antonio to a glorious girl in the "Alamo"
She drew from her girdle a dear little dagger, the sting of a wasp it made me stagger,
One inch to the left, one inch to the right and I wouldn't be speaking here to night,
But she sobbed and swiftly bound her torn rebosa about my wound,
That I quite forgave her – scratches don't count in Texas, down by the Rio Grande.

The air was heavy, the night was hot, I sat by her side and forgot,
Forgot that the herd was taking its rest, forgot that the night was close oppressed,
That the Texas Northern comes sudden and soon, in the dead of night or the blaze of noon,
And let the steeds in their fright take flight and nothing on earth can stop their flight,
And woe to the rider and woe to the steed that falls in front of their mad stampede.
Was that thunder? No by the Lord! I sprang to my saddle without a word,
One foot on mine she leaped behind, away on a wild chase down the wind,
Never was fox hunt so hard, never was steed so little spared,
As we raced for our lives you will see how we fared, in Texas, down by the Rio Grand.

The cattle gained on us and just as I felt for my old six-shooter behind on my belt,
Down came the mustang and down came we clinging together, and what was the rest,
A body that spread itself over my breast, two arms that steadied my dizzy head,
Two lips that close to my lips were pressed, and when I could rise, Laska was dead!!

I dug out a grave a few feet deep and there in earth's arms I laid her to sleep,
And there she lies and nobody knows, the summer sun shines and the winter snows,
The old snake slides, glitters and glides to its nook in the cotton-wood tree,
The buzzard flies on, comes and is gone, stately and bold like a ship at sea,
And I often wonder why I do not care for the things that are and the things that were,
Does half my heart lie buried there, in Texas, down by the Rio Grande.

## THE FOUR SEASONS
### In memory of
Vanessa Anne Pendergast – Oct 13, 1978 - May 3, 1985

Little Vanessa was hit by a school bus and killed – a great tragedy. Her mother Sophia is Frank Gerardi's sister. This poem was written for Sophia and Bill, Vanessa's parents.

SPRING
Birds call and answer in the morning air,
Spring is here, Birds sing.
Crocus in their color show.
Shrubs and trees take on their hue of green
And all things large and small
Hurry to the call of spring.
And you are always near Vanessa,
Yes, you are near

SUMMER
Summer comes
Warm gentle breezes blow
Sun scintillating on gentle streams,
Ocean waves smashing against rocky shores
Cascading their snow-white foam
Petals into the azure sky.
Children playing in fields of green and gold
Casting joyful laughter to the evening sun.
The night is clear
And you are near to us Vanessa dear,
So very near.

AUTUMN
Rainbow colors and trees of gold and brown,
Rivers and streams in autumn tones
Drifting over rocky sandy ways
Humming sounds at eventide
Above the shaded glades.
Fish abounding,
Wild birds sounding,
All the land is fresh and clear.
And you are near Vanessa dear,
Yes always near.

WINTER
Wildlife scatters to their shaded lair,
Birds fly to the warmer clime,
Sun cools and snow appears
Along the mountain line.
The icy winds bring frigid cold,
The winter's grip will all enfold
And sweep the leaves from tall and stately trees,
Leaving the stark reality
That winter is here.
But you will always be to us
So very near Vanessa dear,
So very, very near

FROM THE PARENTS OF
Vanessa Anne Pendergast

Dear Grandpa Coy —

How beautiful your words and how special your heart — I love you and cannot ever tell you how much you mean to everyone in our family —

With love —
Sophia, Bill and Children

October 17, 1994

Dear Grandpa —

I am sending a copy of October 13th's Newport Daily News (the local section) and if you turn to page C2 you will find a 16th Birthday Remembrance of Vanessa with your beautiful poem, The Four Seasons, in her memory —

Thank you Grandpa. You have made this day much less painful for Bill and I and we love you so much for your love and your beautiful words —

I have had calls from friends and they all said the same thing, although they cried while reading your poem, it also filled them with a loving warmth — they all agreed — you are an artist —

## TO THERESE AND BRENDAN – "MY WISH FOR YOU"

When springtime comes
Cool breezes blow – and in
Your garden flowers grow,
All this I wish for you.

In summer time the sun's
Warm glow, fields of green,
Skies of blue – All this I
Wish for you

Trees take on their golden glow,
Streams to the river flow,
Birds sing and seem to know
That autumn is here,
This I wish for you.

When winter comes I wish for you
A happy home with warmth, peace and love,
But most of all I wish for you
God's blessings from above.

2003

## TO DEAREST LITTLE RITA

I knew you as a little girl
So gentle, sweet and fair,
I longed to be a little boy
That with you I may share
My childhood days

A few years pass. I knew you then
In girlhood, and it pleased me so
To watch you with your head erect
And all your sweetness bringing joy.
My heart just leapt for very joy
And made me wish again
That I was just a boy.

A few more years, then womanhood,
These years that passed could never
Such sweet disposition alter.
May one long chain of happiness be yours
Is the heartfelt wish of your much loving
Uncle Walter

*Celebrating my 90th & 91st birthdays in Newport, RI*

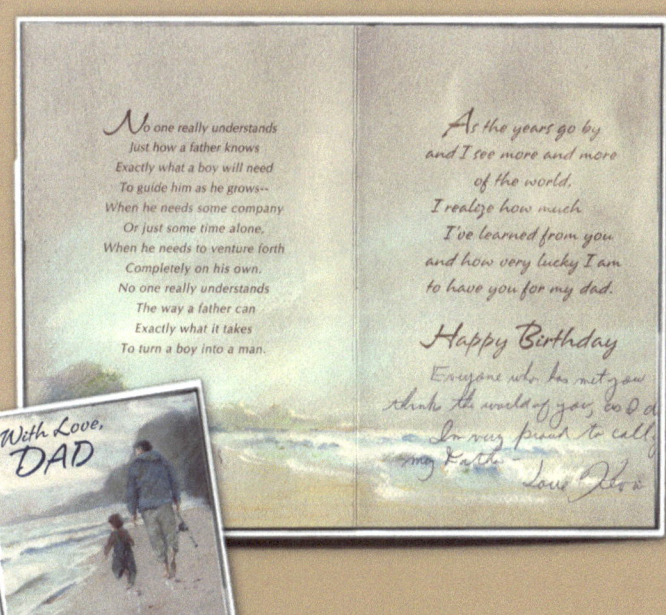

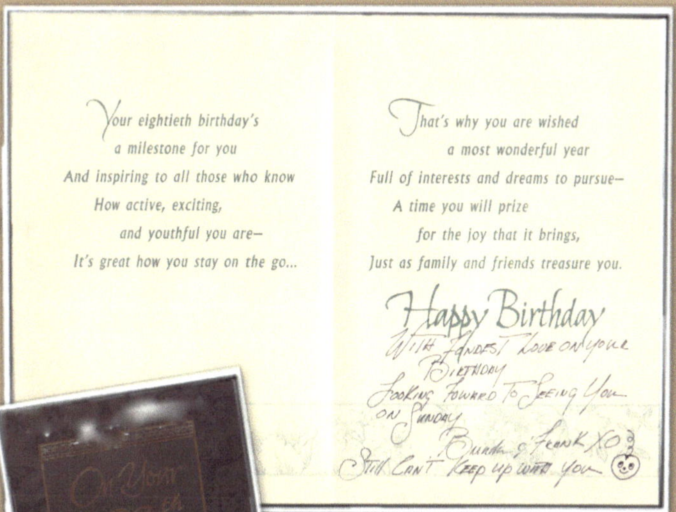

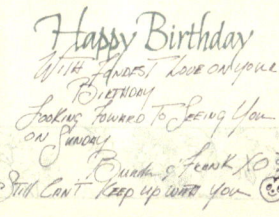

Drawn by my brother in law Tom Hennesy around 1946

To my grandchildren, Richard, Steven, Nicholas, Jeanette, Erin, Michael and my great grandchildren Alexander and Aria. Your life's journey is just starting. Live it well and be kind to each other. Keep love and understanding for others in your heart and may your lives be filled with happy days.

Love,

Grandpa

www.ingramcontent.com/pod-product-compliance
Lightning Source LLC
Chambersburg PA
CBHW040906020526
44114CB00037B/73